USEFUL EXPRESSIONS

in RUSSIAN

FOR THE ENGLISH–SPEAKING TOURIST

Editors: A. Z. Stern — Joseph A. Reif, Ph.D.

·K·U·P·E·R·A·

© 1991 KS-JM Books

Distributed in the United Kingdom by:
Kuperard (London) Ltd.
30 Cliff Road
London NW1 9AG

ISBN 1-870668-71-5

This book is an up-to-date and practical phrase book for your trip to Russia. It includes the phrases and vocabulary you will need in most of the situations in which you will find yourself, and it contains a pronunciation guide for all the material. Some of the phrases occur in more than one section so that you do not have to turn pages back and forth. At the beginning is a basic, general vocabulary with which you should become familiar, and at the end is a list of emergency expressions for quick reference.

The pronunciation of Russian may seem formidable at first, but with the aid of the transcription provided throughout this book you will quickly achieve an easily understandable accent. The transcription should be read as follows:

VOWELS: **a**   as in father when stressed, but more like **o** in off when unstressed

e   as in let

i   as in machine

ı   (without dot) like **i** in hit, but with the tongue retracted a bit

o   as in off

u   like **oo** in boot

Any of the above vowels may form a diphthong with y, e.g., **oy** as in boy.

Vowels, particularly **e**, are often pronounced with a palatal on-glide, indicated here by **y** before the vowel, e.g., nyet "no".

CONSONANTS: **b, d, f, g, k, l, m, n, p, s, t, v,** and **z** as in English.

kh   like **ch** in Scottish lo**ch**

r   is trilled

shch   is a combination of **sh** and **ch** which functions as a single consonant

zh   like **s** in measure

Consonants are sometimes palatalized or "softened" by pronouncing a slight **y** after them. This indicated by an apostrophe ' after the consonant or by **y** in the transcription. Stressed syllables are printed in **boldface**.

CONTENTS

BASIC DICTIONARY	SPISOK SLOV I VIRAZHENIY	СПИСОК СЛОВ И ВЫРАЖЕИЙ
Thank you	spasibo	Спасибо
Thank you very much	balshoye spasibo	Большое спасибо
Please	pozhaluysta	Пожалуйста
Excuse me	izvinitye menya	Извините меня
Never mind	nyevazhno	Не важно
What? What is that?	chto? chto eto?	Что? Что это?
Where? Where is that?	gdye? gdye eto?	Где? Где это?
When? How?	kogda? kak?	Когда? Как?
Which? Why?	kotorıy? pochemu?	Который? Почему?
Is that?	eto li?	Это ли...?
That is not	eto nye	Это не
Yes, no, perhaps	da, nyet, mozhet bit'	Да, нет, может быть
Correct, incorrect	pravil'no, nye pravil'no	Правильно, не правильно
So so	tak syebye	Так себе
Good, bad	kharasho, plokho	Хорошо, плохо
No good, not bad	nye kharasho, nye plokho	Не хорошо, не плохо
There is, there is not (none)	yest', nyet	Есть... нет...

I, you	ya, tı	Я, ты
He, she	on, ona	Он, она
We, you	mı, vı	Мы, вы
They	oni	Они
Mine, yours	moy (maya), vash (vasha)	Мой (моя) ваш (ваша)
Ours, theirs	nashe, ikh	Наше, их, ваше
At my place, at your place	ou menya, ou vas	У меня, у вас
Wet, dry	mokпy, sukhoy	Мокрый, сухой,
Old, new	starıy, novıy	Старый, новый
Pretty, ugly	krasivıy, nye krasivly	Красивый, не красивый
Much, few	mnogo, malo	Много, мало
How many? How much?	skol'ko	Сколько
Cheap, expensive	dyoshevo, dorogo	Дешево, дорого
Very expensive	otchen' dorogo	Очень дорого
Free (of charge)	besplatno	Бесплатно
More, less	bol'she, myen'she	Больше, меньше
Cheaper, more expensive	dyeshevlye, dorozhe	Дешевле, дороже
Heavy, light	tyazhelo, lekhko	Тяжело, легко

2

Now, at the same time as...	syechas, v tozhe samoye vryemya	Сейчас, в то же самое время
During	vo vryemya	Во время
Early, late	rano, pozdno	Рано, поздно
On time, in time	vovryemya	Вовремя,
Here, there	zdyes, tam	Здесь, там
Inside, outside	vnutri, snaruzhı	Внутри, снаружи
Up (stairs), down (stairs)	vvyerkh, vniz	Вверх, вниз
To...	k ...	к ...
Near, far	blizko, dalyeko	Близко, далеко
In front of	pered (vperedi)	перед (впереди)
Behind (after)	za (poslye)	за... (после)
Sky	nyebo	Небо
Sun, moon	solntse, luna	Солнце, луна
Stars	zvyozdı	Звезды
Light, darkness	svyet, tyemnata	Свет, темнота
Heat, cold, warm	zhara, kholod, tyeplo	Жара, холод, тепло
East, west	vostok, zapad	Восток, Запад
North, south	sever, yug	Север, Юг

Rain, snow, wind	dozhd', snyeg, **vye**ter	Дождь, снег, ветер
Earth, mountain, valley	zem**lya**, **ga**ra, da**li**na	Земля, гора, долина
River, bridge	re**ka**, most	Река, мост
Desert, sand	**pus**tınya, pe**sok**	Пустыня, песок
Sea, water, ship	**mor**ye, va**da**, para**khod**	Море, вода, пароход
Country, place	stra**na**, **myes**to	Страна, место
City, village	**go**rod, dye**rev**nya	Город, деревня
Road, street	da**ro**ga, **u**litsa	Дорога, улица
House, flat	dom, kvar**ti**ra	Дом, квартира
Room, door	**kom**nata, dvyer'	Комната, дверь
Key, lock	klyuch', **za**mok	Ключ, замок
Wall, window	st'e**na**, ak**no**	Стена, окно
Roof, steps	**krı**sha, stu**pye**ni	Крыша, ступени
Kitchen, toilet	**kukh**nya, tua**let**	Кухня, туалет
Bed, pillows	kra**vat'**, pa**dush**ka	Кровать, подушка
Blanket, carpet	prostı**nya**, kav**yor**	Простыня, ковер
Table, chair	stol, stul	Стол, стул
Man, woman	muzh**chi**na, **zhen**shchina	Мужчина, женщина

English	Transliteration	Russian
Father, mother	otyets, mat'	Отец, мать
Son, daughter	sın, doch	Дочь, сын
Grandson, granddaughter	vnuk, **vnuch**ka	Внук, внучка
Brother, sister	brat, syes**tra**	Брат, сестра
Uncle, aunt	**dya**dya, **tyo**tya	Дядя, тетя
Husband, wife	muzh, zhe**na**	Муж, жена
Boy, girl	**mal**chik, **de**vochka	Мальчик, девочка
Old man, old woman	sta**rik**, sta**ru**kha	Старик, старуха
To want	kha**tyet'**	Хотеть
I want, You want	ya kha**chyu**, vı kha**ti**tye	Я хочу, вы хотите.
I wanted, you wanted	ya kha**tyel**, vı kha**tye**li	Я хотел, вы хотели
I will want, you will want	ya zakha**chyu**, vı zakha**ti**tye	Я захочу, вы захотите
I do not want	ya nye kha**chyu**	Я не хочу
To visit	pose**shchyat'**	Посещать
I visit, you visit	ya pose**shchya**yu, vı pose**shchya**yetye	Я посещаю, вы посещаете
I visited, you visited	ya pose**til**, vı pose**til'**i	Я посетил, вы посетили
I will visit, you will visit	pose**shchyu** , vı pose**ti**tye	Я посещу, вы посетите
To speak	gava**rit'**	Говорить

5

I speak, you speak	ya gavaryu, vı gavaritye	Я говорю, вы говорите
I spoke, you spoke	ya gavaril, vı gavaril'i	Я говорил, вы говорили
I will speak, you will speak	ya budu gavarit', vı buditye gavarit'	Я буду говорить, вы будете говорить
I do not speak	ya nye gavaryu	Я не говорю
To understand	ponimat'	Понимать
I understand, you understand	ya ponimayu, vı ponimayetye	Я понимаю, вы понимаете
I understood, you understood	ya ponyal, vı ponyal'i	Я понял, вы поняли
I do not understand	ya nye ponimayu	Я не понимаю
To go	khadit' (id-ti)	Ходить (идти)
I go, you go	ya khazhu, vī khoditye	Я хожу, вы ходите
I went, you went	ya khadil, vı khadil'i	Я ходил, вы ходили
I will go, you will go	ya paydu, vı paydyotye	Я пойду, вы пойдете
I do not go	ya nye idu	Я не иду
To travel	yezdit' (yehat')	Ездить, (Ехать)
I travel, you travel	ya yedu, vı yeditye	Я еду, вы едите
I travelled, you travelled	ya yezdil, vı yezdil'i	Я ездил, вы ездили
I will travel, you will travel	ya payedu, vı payeditye	Я поеду, вы поедите
I do not travel	ya nye yedu	Я не еду

6

To stand	stoyat'	Стоять
I stand, you stand	ya stoyu, vı stoyitye	Я стою, вы стоите
I stood, you stood	ya stoyal, vı stoyal'i	Я стоял, вы стояли
I will stand, you will stand	ya budu stoyat', vı buditye stoyat'	Я буду стоять, вы будете стоять
I do not stand	ya nye stoyu	Я не стою
To sleep	spat'	Спать
I sleep, you sleep	ya spl'yu, vı spitye	Я сплю, вы спите
I slept, you slept	ya spal, vı spal'i	Я спал, вы спали
I will sleep, you will sleep	ya budu spat', vı buditye spat'	Я буду спать, вы будете спать
I do not sleep	ya nye spl'yu	Я не сплю
To rest	atdıkhat'	Отдыхать
I rest, you rest	ya atdıkhayu, vı atdıkhayetye	Я отдыхаю, вы отдыхаете
I rested, you rested	ya atdıkhal, vı atdıkhal'i	Я отдыхал, вы отдыхали
I will rest, you will rest	ya budu atdıkhat', vı buditye atdıkhat'	Я буду отдыхать, вы будете отдыхать
I do not rest	ya nye atdıkhayu	Я не отдыхаю

To eat	yest' (**ku**shat)	Есть (кушать)
I eat, you eat	ya yem, vı ye**di**tye	Я ем, вы едите
I ate, you ate	ya yel, vı **ye**li,	Я ел, вы ели,
I will eat	ya **bu**du yest'	Я буду есть,
I do not eat	ya nye yem	Я не ем
To drink	pit'	Пить
I drink, you drink	ya pyu, vı **pyo**tye	Я пью, вы пьете
I drank, you drank	ya pil, vı **pil**'i	Я пил, вы пили
I will drink, you will drink	ya **bu**du pit', vı **bu**ditye pit'	Я буду пить, вы будете пить
I do not drink	ya nye p'yu	Я не пью
To be afraid	ba**yat**sa	Бояться
I am afraid, you are afraid	ya ba**yus'**, vı ba**yi**tyes'	Я боюсь, вы боитесь
I was afraid, you were afraid	ya ba**yal**sya, vı ba**ya**lis'	Я боялся, вы боялись
I will be afraid	ya **bu**du ba**yat**sa	Я буду бояться
You will be afraid	vı **bu**ditye ba**yat**sa	Вы будете бояться
I am not afraid	ya nye ba**yus´**	Я не боюсь,
Don't be afraid	**nye**chevo ba**yat**sa	Нечего бояться
To sit	si**dyet'**	Сидеть
I sit, you sit	ya si**zhu**, vı si**di**tye	Я сижу, вы сидите

English	Transliteration	Russian
I sat, you sat	ya sidel, vı sidyel'i	Я сидел, вы сидели
I will sit, you will sit	ya budu sidyet'	Я буду сидеть, вы будете
	vı buditye sidyet'	сидеть
To hurry	tarapitsa	Торопиться
I am in a hurry	ya taraplyus'	Я тороплюсь
You are in a hurry	vı taropityes'	Вы торопитесь
I hurried, you hurried	ya tarapilsa, vı tarapilis'	Я торопился, вы торопились
I will hurry	ya budu tarapitsa	Я будут торопиться,
I am not in a hurry	ya nye taraplyus'	Я не тороплюсь
To ask for help	prasit' pomoshch'	Просить помощь
I ask for help	mnye nuzhna pomoshch'	Мне нужна томощь
You ask for help	vam nuzhna pomoshch'	Вы просите вам помочь
I asked for help	ya prasil mnye pomoch	Я просил мне помочь,
I am not asking for help	ya nye prashu pomoshchi	Я не прошу помощи
Passport flight	passport, palyot	Паспорт, Полет
Outgoing flight	vılyet	Вылет
Following flight	slyeduyushchiy palyot	Следующий полет
Flight number, suitcase	nomer palyota, bagazh	Номер полета, Багаж
Customs, money	tamozhnya, dyen'gi	Таможня, Деньги

FIRST MEETING; GREETINGS	PERVAYA VSTRYECHYA PRIVETSTVIYA	ПЕРВАЯ ВСТРЕЧА ПРИВЕТСТВИЯ
Hello!	**zdra**stvuitye	Здравствуйте
Good morning	**dob**roye **ut**ro	Доброе утро
Good evening	**dob**rıy **vec**her	Добрый вечер
Good night	spa**koy**noy **no**chi	Спокойной ночи
Welcome!	do**bro** pazh**ha**lovat'	Добро пожаловать
My name is …	**mo**yo **im**ya	Мое имя …
I am from the United-States	ya iz soedi**nyor**ıkh **shta**tov	Я из Соединенных Штатов
I speak only English	ya ga**va**ryu po an**glii**ski	Я говорю по-английски
I am pleased to meet you	**pry**atno pazna**ko**mitsa	Приятно познакомиться
How are you?	kak pozhı**va**yete?	Как поживаете?
Thank you, And how are you?	kha**ra**sho, spa**si**bo	Хорошо, спасибо
How are things?	kak **de**la?	Как дела?
All right	kha**ra**sho	Хорошо
I've come to learn about your country	ya priye**khal** pozna**ko**mitsa **sva**shey stra**noy**	Я приехал познакомиться с вашей страной
I've come on a vacation	ya priye**khal** v **ot**pusk	Я приехал в отпуск

10

Is there someone here who speaks English?	yest li zdyes kto nibud' gavaryashchi po angliiski?	Есть ли здесь кто-нибудь, говорящий по-английски
Yes; No	da, nyet	Да, нет
I speak English	ya gavaryu po angliiski	Я говорю по английский
I speak a little	ya nyemnogo gavaryu	Я говорю немного
Do you understand me?	vi menya panimayete ?	Вы меня понимаете?
I understand a little	ya nyemnogo panimayu	Я понимаю немного
Pardon, excuse me	izvinitye, prostitye menya	Извините
I am sorry	prashu prashchenya	Прошу прощения
It doesn't matter	nye imeyet znacheniya	Не имеет значения
Thank you very much	bal'shoye vam spasibo	Большое вам спасибо
Don't mention it	nye stoit blagadarnosti	Не стоит благодарности
What do you want?	chto vı khatitye?	Что вы хотите?
I would like to visit the city	ya vı khatyel pasetit' gorod	Я бы хотел посетить город
Wait a minute!	padazhditye minutku	Подождите минутку
Come with me!	idyomt'e so mnoy	Идемте со мной
I have to leave now	ya dolzhen seichas uyekhat	Я должен сейчас уехать
Thank you for your attention	spasibo za vnimanye	Спасибо за внимание
Good luck!	schastlivo!	Счастливо!

11

| See you later! | do **skoroy vstre**chi | До скорой встречи |
| Goodbye! | dasvi**dan**ya | До свидания |

HOTEL

I am looking for a good hotel

I am looking for an inexpensive hotel

I booked a room here. Is it ready?

Have you a single room?

A double room?

Have you a better room?

Does the room have a shower?

GASTINITSA

ya **ishchu** kharo**shu**yu gastinitsu

ya is**hchyu** nye dara**gu**yu gastinitsu

ya zaka**zal** zdyes' **no**mer. ga**tov** li on?

yesɩ́ li u vas atdeln1y **no**mer?

nomer na **dvoikh**?

yest' li u vas **kom**nata pa**luch**she?

yest' li v **kom**natye dush?

ГОСТИНИЦА

Я ищу хорошую гостиницу

Я ишу недорогую гостиницу

Я заказал здесь номер, готов ли он?

Есть ли у вас отдельный номер?

... номер на двоих?

Есть ли у вас комната получше?

Есть ли в комнате душ?

With breakfast?	s **zav**trakom	С завтраком
How much is the room?	**skol'**ko **sto**it **no**mer?	Сколько стоит номер?
I should like to see the room	ya kha**tyel** bı pasma**tryet' no**mer	Я хотел бы посмотреть номер
Do you have something	yest́ li u vas **no**mer pa**bol'**she ?	Есть ли у вас номер побольше?
...bigger?		
...Smaller?	...pa**men'**she ?	... номер поменьше?
...Cheaper?	...pade**shev**lye ?	... номер подешевле?
...Quieter?	...pa**ti**she ?	... номер потише?
Will you send for my bags?	pri**ne**sitye paz**ha**luysta moy ba**gazh**	Принесите, пожалуйста, мой багаж
I would like to keep this in the safe	ya bi kha**tyel** khra**nit'** **e**to v **sey**fe	Я бы хотел хранить это в сейфе
Where is the ladies' room?	gdye **zhen**skiy tua**let?**	Где женский туалет?
The men's room?	gdye **mu**zhskoy tua**let?**	Где мужской туалет?
Where is the dining room?	gdye sta**lo**vaya?	Где столовая?
T.V. Room?	gdye tele**vi**zyonaya **kom**nata?	Где телевизионная комната?

English	Transliteration	Russian
Please, wake me at ...	razbuditye menya pazhaluysta v...	Разбудите меня пожалуйста в....
Who's there? Please wait!	kto tam? padazhditye pazhaluysta!	Кто там? Подожите пожалуйста!
Come in!	voyditye!	Войдите!
May I have another towel?	mozhno paluchit' yeshchyo ... adno palatyentse	Можно получить еще одно полотенце?
... another pillow?	...yeshcho adnu padushku	... еще одну подушку?
...another blanket?	... yeshcho adno adeyalo	... еще одно одеяло?
...some hangers?	...neskol'ko veshalok?	... несколько вешалок?
...hot water bottle?	...grelku?	... грелку?
...night lamp?	...nochnuyu lampu?	... ночную лампу?
...thread and needle?	...igolku s nitkoy?	... иголку с ниткой?
...writing paper?	...bumagu dlya pisem?	... бумагу для писем?
...pen?	...ruchku?	... ручку?
Could you cable abroad for me?	pashlitye pazhaluysta telegramu za granitsu?	Пошлите, пожалуйста, телеграмму заграницу?
A vacant room	svabodnıy nomer	Свободный номер
Receptionist	administrator	Администратор

Chambermaid	uborshchitsa	Уборщица
Security Officer	ofitser gosbezo-**pas**nosti	Офицер госбезопасности
Waiter, dining room	ofitsy**ant**, stolovaya	Официант, столовая
Reception room, lift boy	reghistra**tura**, lift**yor**	Регистратура, лифтер
Room key	kl'uch ot **komna**tı	Ключ от комнаты
room number	**no**mer **komna**tı	Номер комнаты
Bed blanket	krava**ı** , ade**yalo**	Кровать, одеяло
Sheet	prosti**nya**	Простыня
Men's toilet	muzh**skoy** tua**let**	Мужской туалет
Ladies' toilet	**zhen**skiy tua**let**	Женский туалет
Toilet paper	tua**let**naya bu**ma**ga	Туалетная бумага

INFORMATION AT HOTEL

INFORMATSIYA POLUCHENNAYA V GOSTINTSE

ИНФОРМАЦИЯ ПОЛУЧЕННАЯ В ГОСТИНИЦЕ

| Is there a taxi station nearby? | **gdye** bli**zhay**shaya osta**nov**ka ta**xi?** | Где ближайщая остановка такси? |
| What is the telephone number? | ka**koy no**mer tele**fo**na? | Какой номер телефона? |

How do I get to :..?	kak mnye papast' v... ?	Как мн пасть в....?
By bus? Where is the bus stop?	avtobusom? gdye astanovka avtobusa?	Автобус Где остановка автобу
Where is the nearest post office?	gdye blizhaishaya pochta?	Где ближ ↓я почта?
Ladies' hairdresser	damskiy parikmakher	дамский парикмахер
Barber	muzhskoy parikmakher	мужской парикмахер
Laundry	prachechnaya	прачечная
Where can I get ↓ ˙˙пack?	gdye ya magu zakusit`?	Где я могу закусить?
Is there a grocery nea˙by?	yest' li pablizasti bakaleinıy magazin	Есть ли поблизости бакалейный магазин?
Where is the Tourist Information Office?	gdye nakhoditsa turistskoye informatsionoye byuro?	Где находится туристское информационное бюро?
Can I have a programme of this week's events?	magu li ya paluchit' programu na etu nyedyelyu?	Могу ли я получить программу на эту неделю?
How can I get to this address?	kak mnye papast' po etomu adresu?	Как мне попасть по этому адресу?
...to the center of town?	...v tsentr gorada?	... в центр города?

How Can get to the shopping district?	...v torgoviy **tsen**tr?	Как мне попасть в торговый центр?
...to a bookshop?	...v **knizhn**iy maga**zin?**	... в книжный магазин?
...to the market?	...na ba**zar?**	... на базар?
...to the exhibitions?	...na **v**ista**v**ku?	... на выставку?
...to the museum?	...v mu**zey?**	... в музей?
...to the theatre?	...v te**atr?**	... в театр?
...to the cinema?	...v ki**no?**	... в кино?
...to a nightclub?	...v noch**noy** bar?	... в ночной бар?
What plays are running this week?	kakiye **pye**si i**dut** na etoy nye**dyel**ye?	Какие пьесы идут на этой неделе?
Which films worth seeing are on this week?	kakiye **fil'**mi stoyt posmo**tryet'** na etoy nye**dyel**ye?	Какие фильмы стоит посмотреть на этой неделе?
Is there a tennis court nearby?	yest' li pabli**z**osti **t**enisnaya plash**chad**ka?	Есть ли поблизости теннисная площадка?
Have you got any mail for me?	yes̃ li dlya me**nya pis'ma?**	Есть ли для меня письма?

English	Transliteration	Russian
Is there a message for me?	yest' li dlya menya soobshchenye?	Есть ли для меня сообщение?
I am going out and will return at …	ya ukhazhu i vernus' v…?	Я ухожу и вернусь в….
I'll leave the hotel tomorrow at …	ya vı-yedu zavtra v…	Я выеду завтра в….
Please make up my bill	prigotovtye pazhaluysta schyot	Приготовьте, пожалуйста, счёт
May I store my luggage here?	magu li ya ostavit' zdyes' svoy bagazh?	Могу ли я оставить здесь свой багаж?
Goodbye	dosvidanya	До свидания

TAXI

TAXI

ТАКСИ

English	Transliteration	Russian
Please call me a taxi.	zakazhıtye mnye pazhaluysta taxi	Закажите мне, пожалуйста, такси
Driver would you please bring my suitcase inside?	shofer, pamagitye, pazhaluysta, zanesti moy chemadan	Шофер, помогите, пожалуйста, занести мой чемодан

Take me to this address,
    please ...
Please drive more slowly

How much is the fare?
Can you come here at ... in
    order to take me back?

atvezitye menya pazhaluysta
    po etomu adresu
yezhaytye medleneye,
    pazhaluysta

skol'ko stoyt proezd?
mozhetye li vı zayekhat' za
    mnoy v...

Отвезите меня, пожалуйста,
    по этому адресу
Езжайте медленнее, пожалуй-
    ста

Сколько стоит проезд?
Можете ли вы заехать за
    мной в..

IN THE POST OFFICE

NA POCHTE

НА ПОЧТЕ

Where is the post office?
Where can I send an overseas
    cable?
Please, give me an overseas
    cable form

How much do I have to pay?
What stamps do I need for
    this letter by ordinary mail?

gdye pochta?
gdye ya mogu paslat'
    telegramu zagranitsu?
dayte mnye pazhaluysta
    blank dlya zagranichnoy
    telegramı
skol'ko s mnya sleduyet?
skol'ko mnye nuzhno marok
    dlya otpravki etovo pis'ma
    prastoy pochtoy?

Где почта?
Где я могу послать
    телеграмму заграницу?
Дайте мне, пожалуйста,
    бланк для заграничной
    телеграммы
Сколько с меня следует?
Сколько марок мне нужно
    для отправки этого
    письма простой почтой?

...by air mail?	...avya pochtoy?	... авиапочтой?
...by registered mail?	...zakaznoy pochtoy?	... заказной почтой?
...by express delivery?	...ekspresom?	... экспрессом?
Please send this registered	poshlitye, pazhaluysta, eto pis'mo zakaznım	Пошлите, пожалуйста, это письмо заказным
Please give me ... post earts to send loeally	daytye mnye... otkrıtok alya mestnoy pochtı	Дайте мне ... открыток для местной почты
Where is the nearest post box in which I put the letter?	gdye nakhoditsa blizhayshıy pachtovıy yashchik?	Где находится ближайший почтовый ящик?
May I have some telephone tokens, please?	mozhno mnye paluchit' neskolko monyet dıya telefona?	Могу ли я получить несколько монет для телефона?
Please, could you get me this number, as I could not get it?	mozhetye li vı soyedinit' menya setim nomerom ya nye mogu nabrat' yevo	Можете ли Вы соединить меня с этим номером, я не могу набрать его.
Please, could you put me through to the International Exchange for this number?	zakazhitye mnye, pazhaluysta, mezhdunarodnıy razgavor po etomu nomeru	Закажите мне, пожалуйста, международный разговор по этому номеру

Please book me a call for tomorrow at ...	zakazhıtye **mnye**, **pazha**luysta, razga**vor** na **zav**tra v...	Закажите мне, пожалуйста, разговор на завтра в...
I've come for my overseas call, booked for ...	ya pri**shol** po **po**vodu mezhduna**zod**novo razga**vo**ra ko**tor**ıy ya za**kaz**al	Я пришел по поводу международного разговора, который я заказал
I'll be waiting here. Please call me when you get the connection	ya padazh**du** zdyes' pozo**vi**tye menya, pa**zha**luysta, kag**da** u vas **bu**dyet svyaz'	Я подожду здесь; Позовите меня, пожалуйста, когда у вас будет связь.
How much do I have to pay?	skol'ko ya pla**chyu**?	Сколько я плачу?
Please, may I have a receipt?	**day**tye mnye, pa**zha**luysta, kvi**tant**siyu	Дайте мне, пожалуйста, квитанцию
Thank you, goodbye	spa**si**bo, dosvi**dan**ya	Спасибо, до свидания

IN THE RESTAURANT

V RESTORANE

В РЕСТОРАНЕ

I am hungry	ya ga**lod**nıy	Я голодный
I am thirsty	ya kha**chyu** pıt'	Я хочу пить
Where is there a good restaurant?	gd'e na**kho**ditsa kha**ro**shıy resto**ran**?	Где находится хороший ресторан?

English	Transliteration	Русский
Waiter	ofi**tsyant**	Официант
Waitress	ofi**tsyant**ka	Официантка
Can I see the menu?	**day**tye mnye pa**zha**luysta men**yu**	Покажите мне, пожалуйста, меню
Breakfast	**zav**trak	завтрак
Lunch	**abed**	обед
Dinner	**uzh**ın	ужин
I would like to order	ya bı kha**tyel** zaka**zat'**...	Я бы хотел заказать ...
Give me this	**day**tye mnye eto	Дайте мне это
Tea with lemon	chay s li**mo**nom,	чай с лимоном,
Tea with milk	chay s mala**kom**	чай с молоком,
Coffee and milk	**kofe** s mala**kom**	кофе с молоком
Turkish coffee	rastvo**rimı**y **kofe**,	растворимый кофе,
Nescafé and	**chyor**nıy **kofe**	черный кофе
Milk, cocoa	ma**lako**, **kaka**o	молоко, какао
Cold, warm, hot	kha**lodnı**y, **tyoplı**y ga**rya**chiy	холодный, теплый, горячий
Cold water, soda water	kha**lodnaya va**da, gazi**ro**vanaya **va**da	холодная вода, газированая вода

English	Transliteration	Russian
Orange juice, grapefruit juice	apel'sinoviy sok	апельсиновый сок
	greypfrutoviy sok	грейпфрутовый сок
Cake, ice-cream	pirozhnoye, marozhenoye	пирожное, мороженное
White beer, black beer	pivo, kvas	пиво, квас
Sweet wine, dry wine	sladkoye vino, sukhoye vino	сладкое вино, сухое вино
Cognac, whisky	konyak, viski	коньяк, виски.
Buttered roll	bulachka s maslom	булочка с маслом
White bread, black bread	byeliy khlyeb, chyorniy khlyeb	белый хлеб, черный хлеб
Rolls		булочки, бублик
Egg, soft-boiled egg	yaitso, yaitso v smyatku,	яйцо, яйцо в смятку,
Omelette, fried egg	yaichnitsa, zharennoye yaitso	яичница, жаренное яйцо
White cheese, yellow cheese	tvarog, sir	творог: сыр
Kefir sour-cream	kefir, smetana	кефир, сметана
Beans	garokh	горох
Sausage, hot dogs	kalbasa, sasiski sbulachkoy	колбаса, сосиски с булочкой?
Vegetable salad	ovashchnoy salat	овощной салат
Salt, oil, sugar	sol', rastitelnoye maslo	соль, растительное масло,
	sakhar	сахар

Pepper, lemon juice	perets limonıy sok	перец, лимонный сок
Olives, pickled cucumber	maslinı, marinovanıye agurtsı	маслины, маринованные огурцы
Herring, pickled fish	selyodka, marinovanaya rıba	селёдка, маринованная рыба
Smoked fish, lakerda	kapchyonaya rıba	копченная рыба
Filleted fish	rıbnoye fil'e	рыбное филе
Baked, filled carp	pechonıy, farshirovanıy karp	печеный, фаршированный карп
Baked, grilled, boiled	pechenoye, zharenoye na rashpere , varyonoye	печеное, жареное на рашпере, вареное
Fried, steamed	zharenoye, varyonoe na paru	жареное, вареное на пару
Chicken, turkey, duck	kuritsa, indyushka, utka	курица, индюшка, утка
Beef, lamb	gavyadina, baranina	говядина, баранина
Liver, tongue	pechyonka yazık	печенка, язык
Steak, shnitzel	otbivnaya, shnitzel	отбивная, шницель
Meat balls	tyeftyeli	тефтели
Beans soup	garokhovıy sup	гороховый суп,
Vegetable soup	ovashchnoy sup	овощной суп
Chicken soup, meat soup	bulyon, myasnoy sup	бульон, мясной суп

Mashed potatoes	kartofelnoye pyure	картофельное пюрэ
Chips	zhareniy kartofel'	жареный картофель
Fruit salad	fruktoviy salat	фруктовый салат
Pudding	puding	пудинг
Glass, bottle, cup	stakan, butilka, chashka	стакан, бутылка, чашка
Spoon, fork, knife	lozhka, vilka, nozh	ложка, вилка, нож
Plate, teaspoon	tareelka, chaynaya lozhka	тарелка, чайная ложка
Serviette, ashtray	salfetka, pepel'nitsa	салфетка, пепельница
Toothpicks	zubochistka	зубочистка
How much must I pay?	skol'ko ya plachu ?	Сколько я плачу?
Change and a receipt, please	daytye pazhaluysta zdachyu i kvitantsiyu	Дайте, пожалуйста, сдачу и квитанцию

GROCERY

	BAKALEYNIY MAGAZIN, BULACHNAYA	БАКАЛЕЙНЫЙ МАКАЗИН, БУЛОЧНАЯ
White bread, brown bread	beliy khlyeb, chorniy khlyeb	белый хлеб, черный хлеб
Milk, kefiz	malako, kefir, prostokvasha	молоко, кефир,
Sour cream, white cheese	smetana, tvarog	сметана, творог
Yellow cheese, salt cheese	sır, (golandskiy sır), brinza	(голландский сыр) брынза

English	Transliteration	Русский
Butter, margarine	**mas**lo, marga**rin**, rastitelnoye	масло, маргарин,
Oil	**mas**lo	растительное масло
Sardines, tuna fish, tuna salad	sardinı, tu**nets**, salat iz tunt**sa**	сардины, тунец, салат из тунца
Olives, eggs	maslinı, **yai**tsa	маслины, яйца
Soup mix	supovıy para**shok** (sukhoy sup)	суповый порошок (сухой суп)
Sugar, honey, salt	**sa**khar, myod, sol'	сахар, мед, соль
Preserved meat	konservirovanoye **mya**so	консервированное мясо

FRUITS AND VEGETABLES

FRUKTI I OVOSHCHI

ФРУКТЫ И ОВОЩИ

English	Transliteration	Русский
Almonds	min**dal'**	миндаль
Apples	**ya**bloki	яблоки
apricot	abri**dos**ı	абрикосы
Banana	ba**nan**	банан
Beans	fa**sol'**	фасоль
Beetroot	**svyok**la	свекла
Cabbage	ka**pus**ta	капуста

26

English	Transliteration	Russian
Carrot	morkov'	морковь
Cauliflower	tsvetnaya kapusta	цветная капуста
Corn	kukuruza	кукуруза
Cucumber	agurets	огурец
Dates	finiki	финики
Eggplant	baklazhan	баклажаны
Figs	figi	фиги
Garlic	chesnok	чеснок
Grapefruit	greipfrut	грейп-фрут
Grapes	vinograd	виноград
Lemon	limon	лимон
Lettuce	salat	салат
Squash	tıkva	тыква
Melon	dınya	дыня
Nuts	arekhi	орехи
Onion	luk	лук
Oranges	apel'sinı	апельсины
Peaches	persiki	персики
Pears	grushı	груши

Peas	garokh	горох
Pepper	perets	перец
Pomegranate	granatı	гранаты
Potatoes	kartofel'	картофель
Radish	rediska	редиска
Rice	ris	рис
Spinach	shpinat	шпинат
Tomatoes	pamidorı	помидоры
Watermelon	arbuz	арбуз

BANK

BANK

БАНК

Where is the nearest bank?

gdye nakhoditsa blizhayshıy bank?

Где находится ближайщий банк?

I have dollars to exchange.

mnye nado pomenyat' dolları?

Мне надо поменять доллары

Will you please change dollars into rubels, for me?

razmenyaytye mnye pozhaluysta, dolları' na rubli

Поменяйте мне, пожалуй-ста, доллары на рубли

Could I have it in small change, please?	razmenyaytye pazhaluysta dyengi v melkikh kupyurakh	разменяйте мне, пожалуйста, деньги в мелких купюрах,
... in large notes?	...krupnıkh kupyurakh	... в крупных купюрах
Could you, please, give me change for this note?	razmenyaytye mnye pozhalyusta eti banknotı	Разменяйте мне, пожалуйста, эти банкноты
Cash, checks	nalichnie dyen'gi, cheki	Наличные деньги, чеки
Clerk, manager	sluzhashchiy, zavyeduyushchıy	Служащий, заведующий
Cash desk, cashier	kasa, kasir	касса, кассир

CLOTHES

ODEZHDA

ОДЕЖДА

I would like to buy...	ya khatyel bı kupit'...	Я хотел бы купить...
My size is my number is	moy razmer..., moy nomer...	мой размер, ... мой номер ...
May I try it on?	mozhno primerit'?	Можно примерить?
This is too short	eto slishkom korotko,	Это слишком коротко,
Too long	slishkom dlinno	слишком длинно
It is too tight, too loose	eto slishkom uzko, slishkom shiroko	Это слишком узко; слишком широко

29

A pair of shorts	short**ı**	шорты
A pair of trousers	**bryu**ki	брюки
Boots	bo**tin**ki	ботинки
Brassiere	byust**gal**tyer	бюстгалтер
Button	**pu**govitsa	пуговица
Cape	pele**rin**a	пелерина
Coat	pal'**to**	пальто
Collar	voro**tnik**	воротник
Cotton material	bu**mazh**naya tkan'	бумажная ткань
Dress	**pla**tye	платье
Gloves	per**chat**ki	перчатки
Hat	sh**lya**pa	шляпа
Handkerchief	noso**voy** pla**tok**	носовой платок
Jacket	zha**ket**	жакет
Ladies' handbag	**dam**skaya **sum**ka	дамская ручная сумка
Leather	**kozh**a	кожа
Linen	be**lyo**	белье
Nylon stockings	ney**lon**ovıye chul**ki**	нейлоновые чулки

English	Transliteration	Russian
Night shirt	nochnaya rubashka	ночная рубашка
Pocket	karman	карман
Pantyhose	kolgotki	колготки
Pajamas	pizhama	пижама
Raincoat	dozhdevik	дождевик
Robe	khalat	халат
Rubber boots	rezinovıye sapogi	резиновые сапоги
Sandals	sandalı	сандали
Scarf	sharf	шарф
Scissors	nozhnitsı	ножницы
Shoe laces	shnurki	шнурки
Shoes	tufli	туфли
Silk	sholk	шелк
Skirt	yubka	юбка
Shirt,	rubashka	рубашка
Slippers	komnatnıye tufli	комнатные туфли
Sports shoes, sneakers	sportivnıye botinki, tapochki	спортивные ботинки, тапочки
Stockings	noski	носки

Sweater	sviter	свитер
Swimsuit	kupalnıy kostyum	купальный костюм
Suit	kostyum	костюм
Synthetic material	synteticheskiy materyal	синтетический материал
Tie	galstuk	галстук
Umbrella	zontik	зонтик
Underpants	kalsonı	кальсоны
Velvet	barkhat	бархат
Undershirt, vest	nizhnyaya rubashka zl.ilyet	нижняя рубашка, жилет
Woolen material	sherstyanoy materyal	шерстяной материал
Zipper	molniya	молния

COLORS

I want a light shade

    Dark shade

    Red, yellow

    Green, blue

TSVETA

ya bı khotyel svyetlıy

otyenok, tyomnıy otyenok

krasnıy zholtıy

zelyonıy, sinıy

ЦВЕТА

я бы хотел светлый оттенок,

    темный оттенок

    красный, желтый

    зеленый, синий

Purple, gray	pur**pur**nıy, serıy	пурпурный, серый
Black, white	**chyor**nıy, **byel**ıy	черный, белый
Brown, pink	ko**rich**nevıy, **ro**zovıy	коричневый, розовый

LAUNDRY

could you please clean my
  suit, coat, sweater?

Please, could you wash and
  iron the shirts and
  underwear?

When will they be ready?

Please also do any necessary
  repairs

The belt of the dress is missing

PRACHECHNAYA

pachistitye, pa**zha**luysta, moy
  kas**tyum**, **ma**yo pal'**to**,
  moy **svi**ter

posti**ray**tye i pag**lad**tye,
  pa**za**luysta, moyl
  ru**bash**ki i bel**yo**

kag**da** eto **bud**yet ga**to**vo?

pochi**ni**tye, paa**ha**luysta, vsyo
  chto **na**do

potye**ryal**sa **po**yas ot **plat**ya

ПРАЧЕЧНАЯ

Почистите, пожалуйста, мой
  костюм, мое пальто, мой свитер

Постирайте и погладьте, пожалуйста, мои рубашки и белье

Когда это будет готово?

Почините, пожалуйста, все
  что надо

Потерялся пояс от платья

BOOKSHOP — KNIZHNIY MAGAZIN — КНИЖНЫЙ МАГАЗИН

BOOKSHOP	KNIZHNIY MAGAZIN	КНИЖНЫЙ МАГАЗИН
I would like to buy …	ya bı khatyel kupit'…	Я хотел бы купить …
…A newspaper	…gazetu	… газету
…A magazine	…jurnal	… журнал
…A guidebook	…putyevodityel`	… путеводитель
…A map of the city	…kartu gorada	… карту города
…A map of the country	…kartu stranı	… карту страны
…Envelopes	…konvertı	… конверты
…A writing pad	…bumagu dlya pisem	… бумагу для писем
…An exercise book,	…tetrad', karandash	… тетрадь, карандаш
…A pencil		
…A fountain pen	…samopishushchuyu ruchku,	… самопишущую ручку,
…A ballpoint pen	…sharikavuyu ruchku	… шариковую ручку
…A refill for the pen	…sterzhen dlya ruchki	… стержень для ручки

AT THE HAIR DRESSER — У ПАРИКМАХЕРА

AT THE HAIR DRESSER		У ПАРИКМАХЕРА
I want to get a hair cut	ya khochyu pastrichsya	Я хочу подстричься
In front, on the sides, behind	speredı, szadi	спереди, с боков, сзади
Shorter, longer	karoche, dlineye	короче, длиннее

Side locks, beard, moustache	baken**bard**ı, bara**da**, ussı	бакенбарды, борода, усы
How long must I wait?	**skol**ko **vry**emyeni ya **dol**zhen zhdat´?	Сколько времени я должен ждать?
A short while, a long time	nye **dol**go, **dol**go	Недолго, долго
I want a shampoo, please	ya bı kha**tyel** po**mı**t' **go**lavu	Я бы хотел помыть голову
The water is too hot	va**da** **slish**kom gar**ya**chaya	Вода слишком горячая
I want a shave	ya bı kha**tyel** pa**brits**a	Я бы хотел побриться
Be careful here!	osto**rozh**nyeye!	Осторожнее!
I want my hair dyed	ya bı kha**tyel**a pak**ras**it' **vol**osı	Я бы хотела покрасить волосы
I want my hair set	ya bı kha**tyel**a ulo**zh**it' **vol**osı	Я бы хотела уложить волосы
Pedicure, Manicure	pedi**kyur** mani**kyur**	Педикюр, маникюр

THE WEATHER

PAGODA

ПОГОДА

What a beautiful day!	**kakoy** chu**dyesn**ı y dyen'!	Какой чудесный день!
Bright, the sun is shining	**yasno**, **svy**etit **sol**ntse	Ясно; светит солнце
Warm, hot, very hot	**tyep**lo, **har**ko ochen' **zhar**ko	тепло, жарко, очень жарко

Chilly, cold	prokhladno, **kho**lodno,	прохладно, холодно,
Very cold	**otchen**` **kho**lodno,	очень холодно
Dry	**su**kho	сухо
Damp, drizzle, it is raining	sıro, ma**ra**sit, dozhd'	сыро, моросит дождь,
Cloudy, foggy	**pas**murno, tu**man**no	пасмурно, туманно
To wear a warm coat	o**dyet**' tyo**plo**ye pal'**to**	Одеть теплое пальто
Raincoat, cape	dozhde**vik**, **kep**ka	дождевик, кепку
Rubber boots	re**zi**novıye sa**po**gi	резиновые сапоги
To take an umbrella,	vzyat' **zon**tik	Взять зонтик

TRANSPORT

TRANSPORT

ТРАНСПОРТ

Bus, train, plane	**av**tobus, **po**yezd, samol**yot**	автобус, поезд, самолет
Underground, express train	me**tro**, **skor**ıy **po**yezd	метро, скорый поезд
Ticket, ticket office	bil**yet**, bil**yet**naya **ka**sa	билет, билетная касса
Driver, steward, stewardess	sha**f**yor, **sty**uard , styuar**des**sa	шофер, стюард, стюардесса
Load / luggage, porter	ba**gazh**, na**sil**shchik	багаж, носильщик
Where is the lost baggage office?	gdye na**khod**itsa **ka**mera khra**nen**iya ?	Где находится камера хранения?

TRAIN, BUS

From where does the train for
 ... leave?

How do I get there?

By train, bus, underground
 (subway)

Where is the ticket office?

At what time does the next
 train leave for ...?

Give me a ticket for ... please

If possible, by the window and
 facing the front

Where can I find a porter?

Please, take the bags to the
 coach

POYEZD, AVTOBUS

kagda atkhodit poyezd v...?

kak ya tuda papadu?

poyezdom, avtobusom, metro

gdye nakhoditsa bilyetnaya
 kasa ?

v kotorom chassu ukhodit
slyeduyushchiy poyezd v...?

daytye mnye, pozhaluysta,
 bilyet v...

yesli vozmozhno, okolo
 akna po khodu dvizheniya

gdye ya magu nayti
 nosil'shchika?

voz'mitye, pazhaluysta, bagazh
 v vagon

ПОЕЗД, АВТОБУС

Когда отходит поезд в...?

Как я туда попаду?

Поездом, автобусом, метро

Где находится билетная
 касса?

В котором часу уходит
следующий поезд в...?

Дайте мне, пожалуйста,
 билет в...

Если возможно, около окна
 и по ходу движения

Где я могу найти
 носильщика?

Возьмите, пожалуйста,
 багаж в вагон

English	Transliteration	Russian
Where is the dining coach?	gdye nakhoditsa vagon restoran?	Где находится вагон-ресторан?
May I open (close) the window?	magu li ya otkrıt' (zakrıt') okno?	Могу ли я открыть (закрыть) окно?
May I smoke?	razhreshıtye zakurit'?	Разрешите закурить?
When does the train arrive at?	kagda poyezd prıbıvayet v...?	Когда поезд прибывает в...?
What bus goes to...?	kakoy avtobus idyot v...?	Какой автобус идет в...?
Where is the bus to ...?	gdye nakhoditsa avtobus, idushchiy v...?	Где находится автобус, идущий в....?
How much is a ticket to ...?	skol'ko stoyt bilyet v...	Сколько стоит билет?
Is this the bus to ...?	idyot li etot avtobus v...?	Идет ли этот автобус в...?
I am looking for this address	ya ishchyu etot adress	Я ищу этот адрес
At which station do I get off?	skazhıtye mnye pozhaluysta gdye soyti ?	Скажите мне, пожалуйста, где сойти?

AIRPLANE

SAMOLYOT

САМОЛЕТ

| By which means of transport do I get to the airport? | na chyom ya magu prayekhaţ v aeroport? | На чем я могу проехать в аэропорт? |

English	Transliteration	Russian
Is there a bus service (taxi) to there?	**khod**yat li tu**da avto**busı ili ta**xi**	Ходят ли туда автобусы или такси?
At what time will I be picked up?	kag**da za mnoy zaye**dut?	Когда за мной заедут?
Which is the nearest bus stop to the airport?	gdye na**kho**ditsa bli**zhay**shaya osta**nov**ka av**to**busa v aero**port?**	Где находится ближайшая остановка автобуса в аэропорт?
at what time should I be there?	v ka**to**rom cha**su** ya **dol**zhen tam bı**t**`?	В котором часу я должен там быть?
At what time does the plane take off?	v ka**to**rom cha**su** ule**ta**yet sama**lyot?**	В котором часу улетает самолет?
When will it arrive?	kag**da** on prile**t**ıt?	Когда он прилетит?
Is there a flight to?	yest' li pa**lyot** v...?	Есть ли полет в...?
What is the flight number?	ka**koy no**mer pal**yo**ta?	Какой номер полета?
I have nothing to declare	u me**nya** niche**vo** nyet dlya dekla**rats**ıy	У меня ничего нет для декларации
This is all I have	eto vsyo chto ou me**nya ime**yetsa	Это все, что у меня имеется,

Please, take my luggage	voz'**mit**ye, pa**zha**luysta, moy ba**gazh**	Возьмите, пожалуйста, мой багаж
May I have a travel sickness pill, please?	**day**tye mnye, pa**zha**luysta, tab**ly**etku ot toshn**ot**ı	Дайте мне, пожалуйста, таблетку от тошноты
May I have a glass of water?	**day**tye mnye, pa**zha**luysta, sta**kan** vodı	Дайте мне, пожалуйста, стакан воды

CAR JOURNEY

PUTESHESTIYE MASHINOY

ПУТЕШЕСТВИЕ МАШИНОЙ

Where can I rent a car?	**gdye ya** ma**gu** vzyat' nap**rok**at mash**ı**nu?	Где я могу взять на-прокат машину?
I have an international driving license	u men**ya ime**yutsa mezhduna**rod**nıye vo**dit**el'skiye pra**va**	У меня имеются международные водительские права
How much is it to rent a car per day?	**skol**'ko stoyet pra**kat** mash**ı**nı v dyen' .?	Сколько стоит прокат машины в день?
What is the additional rate per kilometer?	**skol**'ko **nuzh**no platit' do**ba**vochno za **kazh**dıy, kilo**met**er ?	Сколько нужно платить добавочно за каждый километр?

40

Where is the nearest petrol (gas) station?	gdye nakhoditsa blizhayshaya benzokalonka	Где находится ближайщая бензоколока?
Please, put in ... liters	napolnitye, pazhaluysta, ...litrov	Наполните, пожалуйста.... литров
Check the oil, please	provyertye, pazhaluysta, maslo	Проверьте, пожалуйста, масло,
...the brakes	...tormoza	.... тормоза
...the gear box	...pereklyuchatyel' skorostey	.... переключатель скоростей
Please put water in the battery, radiator	nalyeytye, pazhaluysta, vodi v batareyu, radyator	Налейте, ножалуйста, воды в батарею, радиатор
Change the oil in the car, please	smenitye, pazhaluysta, smazku v mashinye	Смените, пожалуйста, смазку в машине
May I have a road map of the area?	magu li ya poluchit' dorozhnuyu kartu etovo rayona?	Могу ли я получить дорож- ную карту этого района?
Please inflate the tires, the reserve wheel too	nakachaytye, pozhaluysta, shini i takzhe zapasnoye kaleso	Накачайте, пожалуйста, шины и также запасное копесо

Please change the inner tube, the tire	smenite, pazhaluysta, kameru	Смените, пожалуйста, камеру
Please repair the puncture	pochinite, pazhaluysta, prakol	Почините пожалуйста прокол
What is the speed limit?	kakaya predel'naya skorost'?	Какая предельная скорость?
Which is the way to …?	kakoy darogoy yekhat' v…,	Какой дорогой ехать в….,
Is that a good road?	…a eta daroga kharoshaya?	Эта дорога хорошая?
Is there a shorter way?	yest' li bolyeye karotkaya daroga?	Есть ли более короткая дорога?
Which place is this?	kakoye eto mesto?	Какое это место?
Is this the road to …?	eta daroga vyedyot v…?	Эта дорога ведет в…?
Yes, no	da, nyet	Да, нет
Please, go back	pozhaluysta, poyezzhaytye abratno	Пожалуйста, поезжайте обратно
Please go straight on	yedtye pryamo	Едте прямо
Turn to the right (left)	povernitye napravo, (nalevo)	Поверните направо (налево)
Turn to the north, (south, east, west)	povernitye na sever, (yug, vostok, zapad)	Поверните на север (юг, восток, запад)

42

English	Transliteration	Russian
This way	v etu **stor**onu	в эту сторону,
That way	v tu **stor**onu	в ту сторону
How far is it to …?	dal**ye**ko li atsyuda do...?	Далеко ли отсюда до...?
Is it near? (far?)	**bliz**ko li (dal**ye**ko li)	Близко ли (далеко ли)?
Very far?	**otchen'** dal**yeko?**	очень далеко?
There, here	tam, zdyes'	там, здесь
Please show me on the map where are we?	poka**zhit**ye mnye, pa**zha**luysta, na **kar**tye, gdye mı na**kho**dimsya?	Покажите мне, пожалуйста, на карте, где мы находимся?
Where is the place that we want to go to?	gdye na**kho**ditsa to **mes**to **kuda** mı **yed**em?	Где находится то место, куда мы едем
On which road should we travel?	po **kakoy** da**ro**ge mı **dolzh**nı **yek**hat'?	По какой дороге мы должны ехать?

TRAFFIC SIGNS

DOROZHNIYE ZNAKI

Дорожные знаки

Stop!	stop	Стоп!
Caution!	asta**rozh**no	Осторожно!

English	Transliteration	Russian
Dangerous curve	krutoy pavarot	Крутой поворот
Travel slowly	yezzhaytye medleno	Езжайте медленно
Danger!	apasnost'	Опасность!
First Aid	meditsınskaya pomoshch'	Медицинская помощь
Red Cross	skoraya pomoshch'	Скорая помощь
Pharmacy	aptyeka	Аптека
Police	militzya	**Милиция**
No parking	stayanka zapryeshchena	Стоянка запрещена
No crossing	peshekhodnıy perekhod zapryeshchyon	Пешеходный переход запрещен
One-way Street	adnastaroneye dvizheniye	Одностороннее движение
Pedestrain crossing	peshekhodnıy perekhod	Пешеходный переход
Detour	obyezd	Объезд
Men at Work	lyudi rabotayut	Люди работают
Right, Left	napravo, nalievo	Направо, налево
Entrance	vkhod	Вход
Exit	vıkhod	Выход

No Smoking	nye kurit'	Не курить
Information	informatsionoye byuro	информационное бюро
Elevator	lift	лифт
Travel on this road	yezzhaytye po etoy doroge	Езжайте медленно
Take care	**budtye ostorozhnı!**	Будьте осторожны
Crossroad	peshekhodnıy perekhod,	пешеходный переход;
Junction, bridge	perekryostok, most	перекресток; мост
Highway	avtostrada	автострада
Bad road	plakhaya daroga	плохая дорога
Narrow road	uzkaya daroga	узкая дорога
Road under repair	daroga v remontye	дорога в ремонте
Clusty road	nye moshchyonaya daroga	немощенная дорога
Steep incline	krutoy podyom	крутой подъем
Steep decline	krutoy spusk	крутой спуск
Sharp turn	krutoy pavarot	крутой поворот
Blinding light	slepyashchiy svyet	слепящий свет
Children on the road	dyeti na daroge	дети на дороге

GARAGE	GARAZH	ГАРАЖ
Where is a garage nearby?	gdye nakhoditsa blizhayshıy garazh?	Где находится ближайший гараж?
Please check and adjust the brakes	provyertye i ispravtye, pazhaluysta, tormoza	Проверьте и исправьте, пожалуйста, тормоза
Please check the gearbox and adjust the clutch	provyertye, pazhaluysta, karobku skorostey i ispravtye stsepleniye	Проверьте, пожалуйста, коробку скоростей и исправьте сцепление
The engine uses too much oil	motor beryot slishkom mnogo masla	Мотор потребляет слишком много масла
The engine is overheating	motor peregrevayetsa	Мотор перегревается
The radiator needs refilling too often	slishkom chasto prikhoditsa dolivat' vodu v radyator	Спишком часто приходится доливать воду в радиатор
Please check the plugs	provyertye pazhaluysta svyechi	Проверьте, пожалуйста, свечи
Please check the points	...smazochnıye tochki	.... смазочные точки
The car doesn't start well	starter mashını nye v paryadke	Стартер машины не в порядке

Please check the headlight alignment	provyertye pazhaluysta regulirovky svyeta	Проверьте, пожалуйста, регулировку света

REPAIRS

POCHINKA

ПОЧИНКА

Wheel balance	balansirovka kalyos	балансировка колес
Oil change	smena masla	смена масла
Tighten screws	zakrepit' boltı	закрепить бопты
Fill the radiator	napolnit' radyator	наполнить радиатор
Oil the engine	smazat' motor	смазать мотор
Wheel alignment	regulirovka kalyos	регулировка колес
Water for the battery	vada dlya batarey	вода для батареи
The gear is stuck	karobka skorostey zayedayet,	коробка скоростей заедает,
The oil is leaking	maslo vıtekayet	масло вытекает
The part is burnt out	dyetal' sgarela	деталь сгорела
To take a wheel apart	razobrat' kaleso	разобрать колесо
Short circuit	karotkoye zamıkaniye	короткое замыкание

The steering wheel is loose	rulevoye kaleso razbaltalos'	рулевое колесо разболталось
The axle rod is broken	kardanıy val slamalsya	корданный вал сломался
Puncture in the tire	prakol v kalesye	прокол в колесе
Everything is O.K.	vsyo v paryadke	Все в порядке

PARTS OF A CAR

CHASTI MASHINI

ЧАСТИ МАШИНЫ

Battery	batareya	батарея
Brakes	tormoza	тормоза
Carburetor	karbyurator	карбюратор
Clutch	stsepleniye	сцепление
Distilled water	distilirovanaya vada	дистилированная вода
Filter	fil'ter	фильтр
Gear	karobka skarostey	коробка скоростей
Ignition	zazhıganiye	зажигание
Pedal	smazka	смазка
piston	pedal', porshen'	педаль, поршень
Radiator	radyator	радиатор

Spark plugs, spring	svechya zazhiganiya, pruzhina rul'	свеча зажигания, пружина, руль
Steering wheel		
Wheel, wheels	kaleso, kalyosa	колесо, колеса

PHYSICIANS

Where does an English speaking doctor live?	gdye zhivyot doktor, gavaryashchiy po angliyski	Где живет доктор, говорящий по английски?
I need first aid	mnye nuzhna pyervaya pomoshch'	Мне нужная первая помощь
I need an internal specialist	mnye nuzhen vrach po vnutrenim bolezny am	Мне нужен врач по внутренним болезням
Can you recommend a good doctor?	mozhetye li vı parekomendovat' mnye kharoshevo vrachya?	Можете ли вы порекомендовать мне хорошего врача?

TYPES OF DOCTORS

	VRACHEBNIYE SPETSAL'NOSTI	ВРАЧЕБНЫЕ СПЕЦИАПЬНОСТИ
Ear, nose and throat specialist	urach ukho-horlo-nos	врач ухо-горло-нос
Orthopedist	ortoped	ортопед
Surgeon	khirurg	хирург

Pediatrician	**det**skiy vrach (pediator)	детский врач (педиатор)
Gynecologist	**zhen**skiy vrach (gen**ko**log)	женский врач (гениколог)
Dermatologist	**ko**zhnıy vrach	кожный врач
Eye specialist	gla**znoy** vrach	глазной врач
Neurologist	nevropa**to**log	невропатолог
Internal specialist	vrach po ınutrennim baleznyam	врач по внутренним болез- ням
Dentist	zub**noy** vrach	зубной врач

ILLNESSES

BALYEZNI

БОЛЕЗНИ

I have no appetite	ou me**nya** nyet ape**ti**ta	у меня нет аппетита
Nausea	toshno**ta**	тошнота
Infection	in**fek**tsiya	инфекция
Depression	de**pre**siya	депрессия
Cold	prastu**da**	простуда
Vomiting	**rvo**ta	рвота
Pregnancy, pregnant	beremenost', be**reme**naya	беременность; беременная
Contraction	**su**dorogi	судороги

Heart patient	serdechnıy bol'noy	сердечный больной
Fever	temperatura	жар,
Ulcer	yazva	язва

PARTS OF THE BODY

	CHASTI TYELA	ЧАСТИ ТЕЛА
Ankle	ladızhka	лодыжка
Appendix	appenditsıt	артерия
Arm	ruka	рука
Aartery	arteriya	артерия
Back	spina	спина
Bbladder	mochevoy puzır'	мочевой пузырь
Blood	drov'	кровь
Bone, bones	kost' kosti	кость, кости
Breast	grud'	грудь
Chest	grudnaya kletka	грудная клетка
Ear	ukho	ухо
Elbow	lokot'	локоть

English	Transliteration	Russian
Eye, eyes	glaz, glaza	глаз, глаза
Finger	palets	палец
Gland	zheleza	железа
Hand	kist' ruki	кисть руки
Head	galava	голова
Heart	sertse	сердце
Heel	pyatka	пятха
Hip, hips	bedro, byodra	бедро, бедра
Intestine, intestines	kishechnik, kishki	кишечник, кишки
Joints	sustavı	суставы
Kidney, kidneys	pochka, pochki	почка, почки
Knee	kaleno	колено
Leg	naga	нога
Ligament	svyazka	связка
Liver	pechen'	печень
Lungs	lyokhkiye	легкие
Mouth	rot	рот

Muscle	muskul	мускул
Neck	sheya	шея
Nerve, nerves	nerv, nervı	нерв, нервы
Nose	nos	нос
Palm	ladon'	ладонь
Ribs	rebro, ryobra	ребро, ребра
Shoulder	plyechyo	плечо
Skin	kozha	кожа
Spine	spinnoy khrebet	спинной хребет
Stomach	zhıvot	живот
Throat	gorlo	горло
Thumb	bol'shoy palets ruki	большой палец руки
Tongue	yazık	язык
Tooth, Teeth	zub, zubı	зуб, зубы
Tonsil	mindalevidnaya zheleza	миндалевидная железа,
Urine	macha	моча
Vein	vyena	вена

PHARMACY

Where is the nearest pharmacy?

Which pharmacy is on duty tonight?

Have you a medicine for a headache?

Toothache

Iodine, aspirin

Valerian drops

Antiseptic cream

Hot water bottle, Heating pad

Cottonwool

Thermometer

I need first aid

What are the office hours?

APTYEKA

gdye nakhoditsa blizhayshaya aptyeka?

kakaya aptyeka dezhurit etoy nochyu?

yest' li u vas lekarstvo ot galavnoy boli?

zubnaya bol'

yod, aspirin

valeryanoviye kapli

antisepticheskaya maz'

grelka

vata

termometr

mnye nuzhna pervaya pomoshch

kagda ana atkrıta?

АПТЕКА

Где находится ближайшая аптека?

Какая аптека дежурит в эту ночь?

Есть ли у вас лекарство от головной боли?

зубная боль

йод, аспирин

валерьяновые капли

антисептическая мазь

грелка

вата

термометр

Мне нужна первая помощь

Когда она открыта?

TIME	**VREMYA**	**ВРЕМЯ**
What is the time?	kotoгy chas?	Который час?
It is four o'clock	chetıre chasa	Четыре часа
Five minutes past six	pyat' minut sed'movo	пять минут седьмого
Half past five	pol shestovo	пол-шестого
A quarter past seven	chetvert' sed'movo	четверть седьмого
Ten minutes to eight	bez desyati vosyem	без десяти восемь
Morning midday	utro, poldyen'	утро, полдень,
Afternoon	poslye abeda	после обеда
Evening, night	vecher, noch'	вечер, ночь.
Midnight	polnoch	полночь
Today	syevodnya	сегодня
Yesterday	vchera	вчера
The day before yesterday	pazavchera	позавчера
Tomorrow	zavtra,	завтра
The day after tomorrow	poshlyezavtra	послезавтра
A second, hour	sekunda, chas	секунда, час
Quarter of an hour	chetvert' chasa	четверть часа

English	Transliteration	Russian
Half an hour	pol chasa	полчаса,
Forty minutes	sorok minut	сорок минут
Day, days	dyen', dni	день, дни,
Week, weeks	nyedelya nyedeli	неделя, недели
Month, months	myesyats myesyatsı	месяц, месяцы,
Year, years	god, dodi	год, годы
Period of … years	period v… let	период в… лет,
In a month	v myesyats	в месяц
Early, I am early	rano, mnye yeshchyo rano	рано, мне еще рано
Late, I am late	pozno, ya apazdal	поздно, я опоздал

DAYS OF THE WEEK	DNI NEDELI	ДНИ НЕДЕЛИ
Sunday, Monday	voskresenye, ponedel'nik	воскресенье, понедельник
Tuesday, Wednesday	vtornik, sreda	вторник, среда
Thursday, Friday	chetverg, pyatnitsa	четверг, пятница
Saturday	subota	суббота

MONTHS	**MESYATSI**	**МЕСЯЦЫ**
January, February	yan**var'**, fev**ral'**	январь, февраль
March, April	mart, ap**ryel'**,	март, апрель,
May, June	may yun'	май июнь,
July, August	, yul', **avgust**	июль, август
September, October	sen'**tyabr'**, ok**tyabr'**	сентябрь, октябрь
November, December	no**yabr'**, de**kabr'**	ноябрь, декабрь

SEASONS	**VREMENA GODA**	**ВРЕМЕНА ГОДА**
Spring, Summer	ves**na**, **le**to	весна, лето,
Autumn, Winter	**o**syen', zi**ma**	осень, зима

NUMBERS	CHISLA	ЧИСЛА
One, two	**adin, dva**	один, два
Three, four	**tri,** chetıre	три, четыре
Five, six	pyat', shest'	пять, шесть
Seven, eight	sem', **vosyem'**	семь, восемь
Nine, ten	**devyat', des**yat'	девять, десять
Eleven, twelve	**adin**atsat', dvenatsat'	одиннадцать, двенадцать
Thirteen, fourteen	**tri**natsat', chetır**nat**sat'	тринадцать, четырнадцать
Fifteen, sixteen	pyat**natsat'**, shest**natsat'**	пятнадцать, шестнадцать
Seventeen, eighteen	sem**natsat'**, vosem**natsat'**	семнадцать, восемнадцать
Nineteen, twenty	devyat**natsat'**, **dvat**sat'	девятнадцать, двадцать
Twenty-one	**dvat**sat' a**din,**	двадцать один,
Twenty-two	**dvat**sat' dva	двадцать два
Thirty	**tri**tsat'	тридцать
Forty	**sorak**	сорок
Fifty	pyatde**syat**	пятьдесят,
Sixty	shesde**syat**	шестьдесят,
Seventy	**sem**desyat	семьдесят

English	Transliteration	Russian
Eighty	vosemdesyat	восемьдесят
Ninety	devyanosto	девяносто
One hundred	sto	сто
One hundred and one	sto adin	сто один,
Two hundred	dvesti	двести
One thousand	tisyacha,	тысяча,
One thousand and one	tisyacha adin	тысяча один
Two thousand	dvye tisyachi	две тысячи
Two thousand and one	adin	две тысячи один
One million	milyon	миллион
One billion	bilyon	биллион

EMERGENCY EXPRESSIONS

Help!	pamagite!	Помогите!
Thief!	vor!	Вор!
Stop, thief!	astanavitye vora!	Остановите вора!
Don't touch me!	nye trogaytye menya!	Не трогайте меня!
Call the police!	vizovitye militsiyu!	Вызовите милицию!
I've lost my way.	ya poteryal darogu	Я потерял дорог
How do I get to this address	kak ya magu papast' v. etot adres?	Как я могу попасть по этому адресу?
I don't feel well.	ya sebya plokho chustvuyu	Я себя плохо чувствую
Call a doctor!	vizovitye vracha!	Вызовите врача!
Call a taxi!	vizovitye taxi!	Вызовите такси!
Take me to a first-aid station.	atvyezitye menya na stantsiyu skoroy pomoshchi!	Отвезите меня на станцию скорой помощи.
Take me to the hospital.	atvezitye menya v bal'nitsu!	Отвезите меня в больницу
Take me to a doctor.	atvyezitye menya k doktaru!	Отвезите меня к доктору

VIRAZHENIYA CHREZVICHAYNOVO POLOZHENIYA

ВЫРАЖЕНИЯ ЧРЕЗВЫЧАЙНОГО ПОЛОЖЕНИЯ